MINECRAFT

First published in Great Britain in 2025 by Farshore

An imprint of HarperCollins*Publishers*
The News Building, 1 London Bridge Street, London SE1 9GF
www.farshorebooks.co.uk

HarperCollins*Publishers*
Macken House, 39/40 Mayor Street Upper,
Dublin 1, D01 C9W8, Ireland

This book is an original creation by Farshore
© 2025 HarperCollinsPublishers Limited

Written by Tom Stone
Additional illustrations by George Lee
Special thanks to Sherin Kwan, Alex Wiltshire, Lauren Marklund,
Kelsey Ranallo and Milo Bengtsson

MOJANG
STUDIOS

ISBN 978 0 00 853731 9
Printed in Italy
1

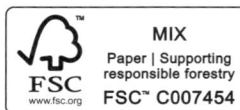

MIX
Paper | Supporting
responsible forestry
FSC™ C007454
FSC
www.fsc.org

This book contains FSC™ certified paper and other controlled
sources to ensure responsible forest management.

For more information visit: www.harpercollins.co.uk/green

MINECRAFT

SURVIVAL CHALLENGES

THE ADVENTURE EDITION

MOJANG STUDIOS

CONTENTS

WELCOME, SURVIVORS!

Minecraft may look cozy and inviting, but we all know that it can be a battle to survive! In this devious collection, Minecraft experts have compiled a series of exciting challenges to take on alone or with your friends. Some are tough, some are brutal and some are so much fun that the creators of this book can't think about them without bursting into laughter!

Maybe you play Minecraft to meet cute mobs or to defeat dangerous creatures. Perhaps you simply love to craft, or have always wondered how long you could survive without crafting anything? Whatever you love doing, this book has challenges that will improve your skills and inspire fun new ways to play the game! Now, are you ready for your first challenge? Turn the page and get started!

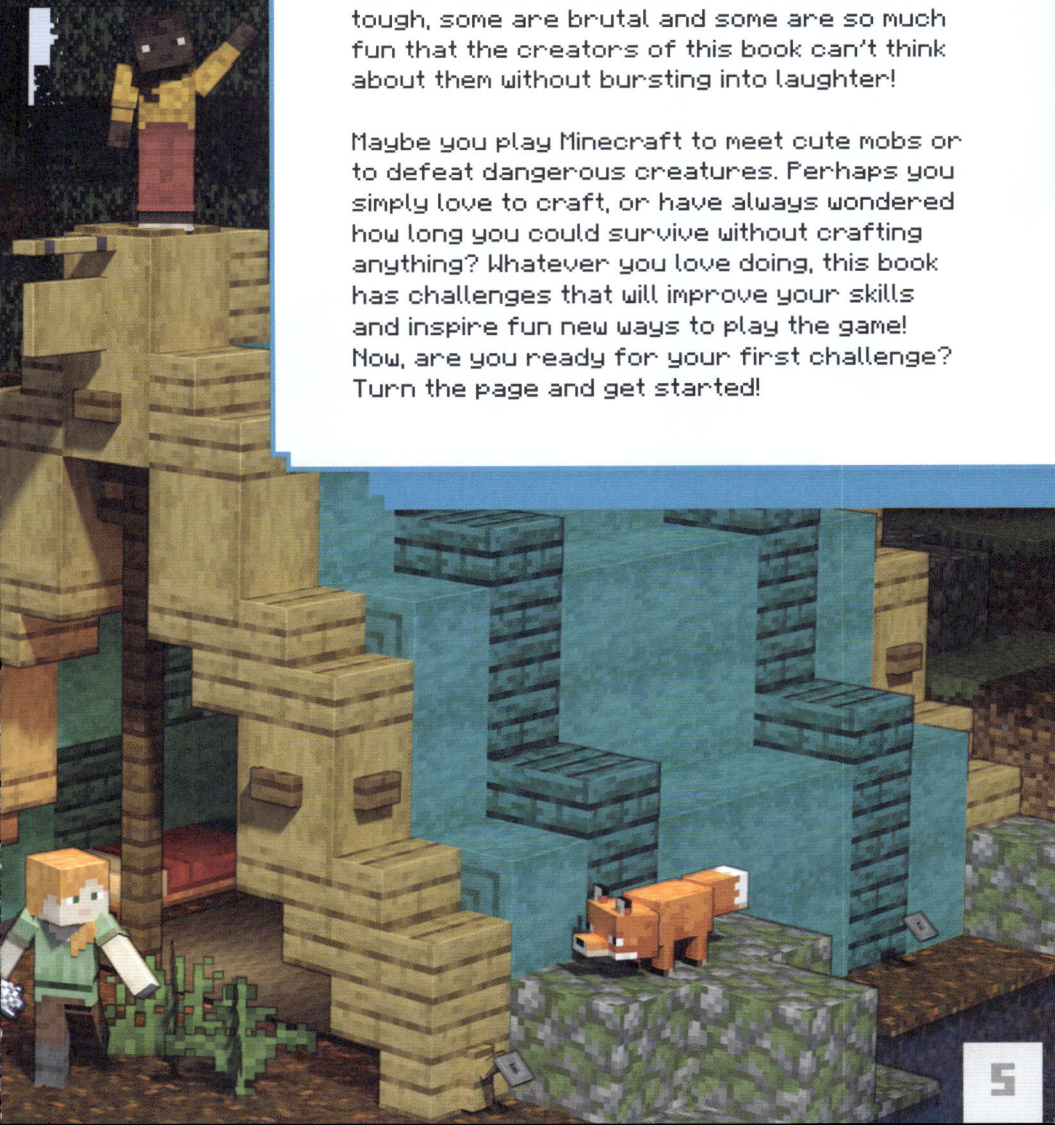

CHALLENGE BASICS

SURVIVAL SPECIALIST

Unless otherwise specified, the challenges in this book are designed to be played in Survival mode. To complete them, you may only use the items specified in each challenge or shown in the icon bar. Some have no restrictions – in those you can gather or craft any items you want!

GET CREATIVE

If a challenge involves using certain blocks or having a structure or map ready to go, feel free to make it or get what you need in Creative mode and then switch back to Survival. You can swap between the two in the settings menu!

HOW WILL YOU RANK?

Every challenge has targets to hit and rankings to try to reach. So if one challenge involves hunting mobs, the lowest rank will be copper, but you can work your way up to iron, then diamond, and finish with netherite. You can also take it in turns with friends to see who can score the best rank!

TOP TIPS

Don't worry, we won't just set you a gruelling challenge and sit back, giggling, while you fail to complete it. Not at all. You'll find lots of tips, tricks and hints throughout the book. So if you're having trouble with a challenge, consult this book for the advice you need to master it!

PERFECT MATCH

Unless you love Minecraft more than we do, there's a chance not every challenge will appeal to you. The great thing about the game is that there's something for everyone. If you're into exploring, we've shown which challenges are best for you. If you prefer to draw your sword and go hunting, we'll let you know what challenges you should try. This is all about having fun, whether playing alone or with some friends!

HAVE FUN!

Want to tweak the challenges so they're more your style? Go for it! Maybe the solo challenges we've created will inspire you to create your own competitive timed challenges with friends? This book is all about finding fun new ways to play Minecraft that suit you. Put your own spin on them all! Turn the page to get started!

AUTOMATIC DEFENCES

Got your hands full fighting hostile mobs? Hrm, wouldn't it be better to build some defences and free your hands for other essential uses, such as mining or crafting? Dispensers are a great way to defend your base, but these challenges will put your skills to the test.

LONE DISPENSER

Dispensers are brilliant for firing arrows at mobs. Simply place a dispenser, with a pressure plate 2 blocks in front of it, then connect them with redstone dust. Fill your dispenser with arrows to complete the trap. Now all you have to do is trick as many hostile mobs as you can to stand on the pressure plate. Can you make it until dawn without returning to your base and using this trap as your only defence?

TOP TIP

Most hostile mobs will make their way towards you, so try tricking them into activating your traps. Move close to the pressure plates and stand on the opposite side so they walk over it!

HOW WILL YOU RANK?

Copper	Survive three minutes
Iron	Survive five minutes
Diamond	Survive the whole night
Netherite	Survive for three nights

Players	Difficulty	Perfect For	Items
1		Strategizers	

LONE DISPENSER, FEWER ARROWS

For this next challenge, we want you to survive the night with a dispenser and use as few arrows as possible. You may not use weapons or armour! We hope you like running around a dispenser while zombies chase you!

Players	Difficulty	Perfect For	Items
1		A truly brave player	

DEFEND THE DISPENSER

Place a dispenser, redstone dust and a pressure plate, but this time put a fire charge in your dispenser. Now build a stack of TNT in front of it. If the pressure plate is triggered, the dispenser will shoot the fire charge at the TNT, causing a huge explosion. Use any weapons you choose, and stop the hostile mobs from stepping on the pressure plate and setting off the trap!

Players	Difficulty	Perfect For	Core Items
1-2		Mob fighters	

COLLECT PASSIVE MOBS

You'll encounter passive mobs across almost all the biomes of the Overworld. Some are common, some are rare, but all of them can have an impact on your game! Many have benefits, including providing food to eat, wool to make a bed and some can even keep hostile mobs away from you!

Players	Difficulty	Perfect For	Items
1		Passive mob lovers	

COLLECT

In this zookeeper challenge, you must head out into the Overworld to collect passive mobs. For the highest rankings, you'll need to build a sanctuary for them to live in and bring back as many as possible! Equip anything you need and get started.

HOW WILL YOU RANK?

Copper

Collect three passive mobs

Iron

Collect five mobs including one water-based mob

Diamond

Collect every passive mob

Netherite

Collect every passive mob and build separate enclosures for each

Turn over for more →

BUILD PENS

Before you collect any of the mobs, you'll need somewhere to put them! Build several wide outdoor pens with fences so they can't escape, but be sure foxes aren't in the same pens as chickens. Build a large pond nearby for any aquatic mobs.

ITEMS TO USE

Did you know that different mobs are attracted to specific items? Hold wheat to make cows, mooshrooms and sheep follow you. Carrots lure pigs and rabbits, seeds attract chickens, seagrass tempts sea turtles, slimeballs attract frogs and spider eyes entice armadillos. Failing that, you can also use a lead!

IN THE WATER

Throw away that fishing rod. The challenge is to collect the mobs, not defeat them! Use a water bucket to scoop mobs out of the sea without harming them. You'll soon have a salmon, pufferfish, tropical fish, cod, axolotl and squid. Wait, a bucket won't work on a squid – but a minecart will!

TAMING

Taming some mobs will cause them to follow you. You can tame a wolf by feeding it bones. Horses can be tamed by mounting them – but prepare to be thrown off countless times before they become tame. Feeding a horse golden apples or golden carrots will help speed up the process!

TRUST

Some mobs can't be tamed, but you can gain their trust. For foxes, you'll need to feed them sweet berries or glow berries so they enter love mode. Once they produce a baby fox, feed it berries and it'll grow up to trust you. You can gain an ocelot's trust by feeding it raw cod or salmon!

HOW CAN PASSIVE MOBS HELP YOU SURVIVE?

Keeping passive mobs nearby can benefit you in many ways!

CAT OR OCELOT
Creepers will flee from any cat or ocelot within a 6-block range, making them a unique method to defend areas of your base.

FOX OR WOLF
Keep a tamed wolf or fox nearby. They will actually attack many of the hostile mobs that could cause you harm.

PARROT
Parrots will often imitate the sounds of many hostile mobs that are approaching, giving you advanced warning!

DOLPHIN
Swimming within a 9-block radius of a dolphin grants you Dolphin's Grace. This effect allows you to swim faster in water!

COW
If you need lots of books for enchanting, cows are a great source of leather. Drinking their milk will also remove nasty status effects.

HIDE AND SEEK

Hiding is essential to survival, as anyone who's accidentally stayed out past sundown will tell you! These challenges will test your abilities to stay hidden and to sniff out anyone sneaking around. You're not reading this aloud are you? Shhh, someone might find you!

HIDE AND SEEK ADVENTURE MAP

In Creative mode, use anything you choose and build a base with two floors. Include lots of good hiding places, because you're going to put the game in Adventure mode, which means players can't mine blocks or place anything to hide behind! Multiple floors will give players a chance to run around and move positions while the seeker explores.

TOP TIP

Give your adventure map a theme! Adding some decorations will make your map a more believable and immersive experience for your players.

HOW WILL YOU RANK?

Copper	Find one player
Iron	Find two players
Diamond	Find all players
Netherite	Find all players in one minute or less

Players	Difficulty	Perfect For	Items
2-4		Seekers	Any

MAPS WITH TRAPS

Now, make a larger map with traps to catch out both the hiders and the seeker. Place dispensers full of arrows or fire charges and connect them to a tripwire using redstone. For extra peril, include doors that lead to pits of lava and rooms full of hostile mobs!

Players	Difficulty	Perfect For	Items
2-4	■■■	Risk takers	Redstone traps

HIDE AND SHRIEK

Build a vast map and then place four chests in it, each with an Ender pearl inside. The first player to seek out all four Ender pearls wins. Too easy? Not really, because you're also going to use a spawn egg to spawn a warden to act as the seeker while you all search. Gulp!

TOP TIP

Start your players on a different floor to the warden. It's not fun or fair if they are caught straightaway!

Players	Difficulty	Perfect For	Items
2-4	■■■	Quiet players	⬡

SKY BLOCK CHALLENGES

Not great with heights? Er, you might want to skip these two pages. Everyone else, welcome to the three airborne challenges that'll make you wish you'd bothered to find a pair of elytra wings! Read on for some adventures that'll really test the air up there!

BUILD A SKY HOME

You could play in Creative mode to build a sky home – but that would be too easy. Put your skills to the test by racing to gather resources and craft a home 50 blocks high within the times given in the rankings. Your sky home must have a door, four walls, a roof and a bed.

TOP TIP

Use dirt blocks or another common block to build yourself a spiral staircase that goes up and up until you're at least 50 blocks above the ground. Just watch your step!

HOW WILL YOU RANK?

Copper	Build your sky home in 20 minutes
Iron	Build your sky home in 15 minutes
Diamond	Build your sky home in 10 minutes
Netherite	Build your sky home in 5 minutes

Players	Difficulty	Perfect For	Items
1		Builders	

16

SKY WALKER

Can you travel through the sky block by block? Stuff as many blocks into your inventory as possible (2304!) then build a bridge in front of you as you walk. You won't fall off if you sneak, so this isn't allowed. This challenge has sent many adventurers plummeting to their doom. Will you survive long enough to use all of your blocks?

Players	Difficulty	Perfect For	Items
1		Builders	

PHANTOM PAIN

Start in Creative mode and build a 12x12 platform in the sky. Use spawn eggs to summon as many phantoms as you can bear! Equip yourself and your friends with any weapons and armour before switching to Survival mode. Now see who can defeat the most phantoms and survive the longest.

TOP TIP

You can select spawn eggs from your inventory in Creative mode. This challenge is best played in rounds. Start with just one phantom to fight. Then two, then three, and so on.

Players	Difficulty	Perfect For	Items
2+		Mob fighters	

POTION EFFECTS

Some of Minecraft's potions can be hugely helpful! But we're not talking about those ones on these challenging pages. Nope, we're playing with negative potions here! Let's see how good you are at Minecraft when you've taken some risky sips of these nasty drinks ...

SLOWPOKE

The potion of Slowness slows you down to the point where even sea turtles are speeding past you. Plus it narrows your field of view. Sounds like the perfect potion for a tough survival challenge! Using any weapons and armour, can you defeat some of Minecraft's toughest foes while under its slow effects?

TOP TIP

There aren't any good sides to drinking a potion of Slowness, but there are ways to help survive its effect! You can use armour and equip shields to block hostile blows, and use any weapon you choose!

HOW WILL YOU RANK?

Copper	Defeat a zombie
Iron	Defeat a skeleton
Diamond	Defeat an Enderman
Netherite	Defeat an evoker

Players	Difficulty	Perfect For	Items
1		Patient players	

SPEED RACERS!

A potion of Swiftness increases your speed and jump distance by 40%, and can improve your field of view – which is how much of the world is visible as you play. It's the perfect potion for a fast-paced race! Build a starting line and a beacon for you and a pal to race towards, then glug down your potions and get racing!

Players	Difficulty	Perfect For	Items
2+	None	Racers	

LUCKY DIP

In Creative mode, find an island and spawn lots of hostile mobs. Then place chests everywhere and put a potion in each one. Put useful potions in half of them, such as Strength or Healing. In the others, place unhelpful ones, such as Poison and Decay. Switch to Survival and have friends fight mobs on your island. If they want a potion, they'll have to risk opening a chest, and they have to drink whatever potion they find!

TOP TIP

Try the island a few times yourself to make sure it's got a manageable amount of mobs on it. For example, multiple wardens would be a bit extreme. We'd also recommend banning players from battling each other. Let's keep this mob hunt civilised, people!

Players	Difficulty	Perfect For	Items
2+	▦▦▦	Risk takers	

START IN THE NETHER

The Nether is a hostile environment where survival is a challenge for even the most experienced players. As perilous as it can be, if you can spend time in this wasteland, you can thrive just about anywhere! Taking on this challenge will change the way you approach Minecraft.

Players	Difficulty	Perfect For	Items
1		Extreme survivalists	None

SURVIVE

Visiting the Nether unarmed is about as smart an idea as trying to hug a creeper. We want you to try starting there with nothing in your inventory ... no food, no armour, no weapons, no gold to placate piglins – and you can't simply hide! Turn the page for some valuable tips!

TOP TIP

You might start with nothing and find it hard to craft any weapons, but there is a way. If you find either a crimson forest or a warped forest, you can harvest crimson or warped stem – which can be used as a wood substitute!

HOW WILL YOU RANK?

Copper
Survive for five minutes

Iron
Survive for 10 minutes

Diamond
Survive for 15 minutes and defeat a mob

Netherite
Survive for 20 minutes and discover two biomes

Turn over for more →

LOCATION

Your initial world spawn point will always be in the Overworld. So start in Creative mode and build a Nether portal (you'll need 10 obsidian blocks). Then use a flint and steel to activate the portal. Change from Creative to Survival, then jump back in. Good luck. You'll need it!

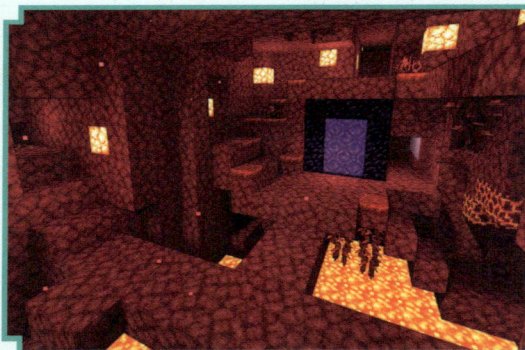

EXPLORING

Netherrack won't drop as a block when broken unless you use a pickaxe. You can still break it, so you can bash paths to go up and down levels. Many spaces in the Nether are enclosed, so creating your own tunnels will offer you a passage and help avoid hostile mobs, such as piglins.

COMBAT

Fighting piglins and zombified piglins is tough without weapons, but your punches will knock them back. Try hitting them down big drops, which will give you valuable time to escape them. Or knock them into lava, which will totally end their pursuits!

ON THE RUN

Surrounded by ghasts, magma cubes, Endermen, piglins, hoglins and more? Then stop reading this and run! When you've got little more than your blocky fists to defend you, sometimes it's best to rely on your legs. Just watch your step – there's danger everywhere!

EATING

Zombified piglins drop rotten flesh. It's not an ideal meal, considering the high chance of it inflicting the Hunger effect, but it'll still help restore some health. If you see any hoglins (found in crimson forest biomes) they drop raw porkchops when defeated but achieving this without a weapon will be a difficult and dangerous task!

NEED A LITTLE EXTRA HELP?

If you're struggling to survive, these quick tips might help ...

FIRE FISTS
If a netherrack block is on fire in the Nether, it can burn forever unless you punch it. But be warned, if you walk over it you'll be burned!

PORTALS
Ruined portals may have chests next to them with supplies. You might find food, so be sure to search around any portals you find!

GHASTS
These floating mobs will shoot exploding fireballs at you. The explosions will also hurt hostile mobs, so use these to defeat them!

ONE-ON-ONE
It's tough, but you can defeat piglins empty-handed if you're fighting one-on-one. Two? Three? Forget about that and just run!

PERSIST!
This is a seriously tough challenge! You're going to perish a lot, but some biomes are safer than others, such as a warped forest, if you can find one!

BE A VILLAGE MAYOR

Found a village? Go ahead and elect yourself mayor! But being mayor isn't all wearing sashes and enjoying fancy dinners. You're also going to need to make your village the best in the Overworld. Complete these challenges and your popularity will soar!

GET DEFENSIVE

It's no fun when your villagers aren't happy … and you must protect them from a village raid! Craft some iron golems (using four iron blocks and a pumpkin), then dig lava moats and place dispenser traps. Place them carefully, you don't want innocent villagers to step on them. When you're ready, trigger the raid!

TOP TIP

You must obtain an ominous bottle from a trial chamber or by defeating an illager captain. Drink this to receive the effect, then enter a village.

HOW WILL YOU RANK?

Copper
Survive the raid

Iron
Survive the raid and only lose three villagers

Diamond
Survive the raid without losing any villagers

Netherite
Survive the raid without having to fight

Players	Difficulty	Perfect For	Items
1		Strategizers	

BOOM TOWN

You're making your villagers live in standard homes and walk on grass blocks made of dirt? For shame! Bulldoze those unworthy dwellings and rebuild a village forged from the fanciest blocks you can gather in Survival mode! Is it vain and pointless to pave the streets with gold blocks? Yes, but you can!

Players	Difficulty	Perfect For	Items
1	◼◼◼	Money Bags	◼ ◼ ◼ ◼

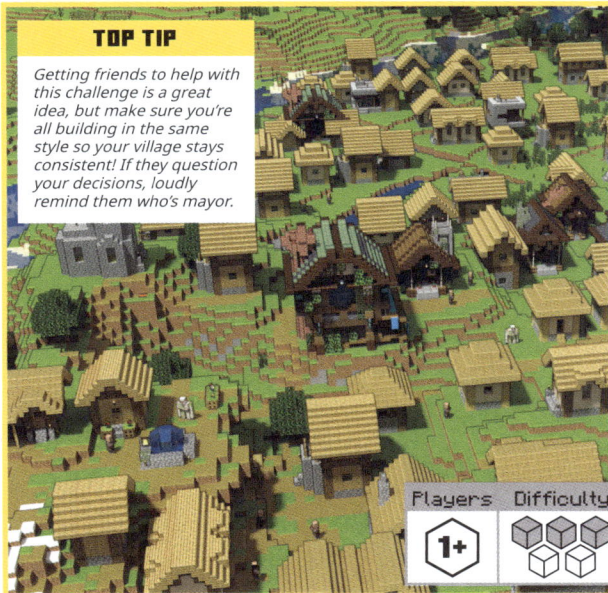

EXPAND!

If village life is too small for an ambitious player like you, it might be time to build a city! Expand your area with stylish new homes, villagers and buildings until it's a sprawling metropolis! You must gather all the materials in your Survival mode game. People will be pleading to join your server and move into your impressive city!

Players	Difficulty	Perfect For	Items
1+	◼◼◼	Builders	◼ ◼

BITE-SIZED CHALLENGES 1

Pressed for time? Only got a few minutes free to play Minecraft before dinner is ready? Not a problem. These time-conscious challenges can be conquered in just a few minutes. But be warned: they might be quick to complete, but they'll take a long time to master!

TIMBER!!!

Most adventures start with you breaking trees to gather wood – it's one of the most useful resources in the game. How many trees can you fell in just five minutes? Begin a timer and start chopping some wood! Every block of the trunk has to be mined for a tree to count so aim for smaller trees first! Start empty handed, but craft a tool if you choose.

TOP TIP

You can't start with any tools, but you can use the wood you're mining to forge a wooden pickaxe! Is it worth taking the time out from tree-punching to craft a tool though?

HOW WILL YOU RANK?

Copper	
8 trees	
Iron	
12 trees	
Diamond	
18 trees	
Netherite	
An amazing 25 trees	

Players	Difficulty	Perfect For	Items
1-4	■■■□□	Lumberjacks	None

FIGHT NIGHT

The whole point of your first day in Minecraft is to prepare for and survive the horrors of night. But what if you didn't do any prep at all? For this challenge, we want you to survive a night using nothing but your fists. You'll never play unprepared again!

Players	Difficulty	Perfect For	Items
1		Fighters	None

GOLD DIGGER

Ever dreamed of getting rich quick? Of course you have! Put that dream to the test by seeing if you can gather any rare metals before night falls in one day. Start a new game and wait for sunrise, then race your friends to craft a pickaxe and go mining. You need to bring your prize back to the surface to win!

TOP TIP

Rare resources, such as iron or diamond, can be valuable crafting ingredients. Use them to make tools, weapons and armour that have higher durability levels.

Players	Difficulty	Perfect For	Items
1-4		Miners	

MINING CHALLENGES

Minecraft isn't called JustStayOnTheSurfaceEatingCakeCraft for a reason – mining is half of what the game's all about! That said, going underground is one thing, but staying there for any length of time will test all of your caving talents!

MINE TIME

Go underground and see how long you can stay there! The longer you remain and the more you can achieve, the better you will rank. Fill your inventory with tools and supplies, and read on for some guidance!

Players	Difficulty	Perfect For	Items
1		Underground enthusiasts	

HOW WILL YOU RANK?

Copper

Stay below ground for one day

Iron

Stay below ground for three days and gather 30 raw iron

Diamond

Stay below ground for five days and find five diamonds

Netherite

Find the deep dark and survive encountering the warden

Turn over for more

STAIRCASE TO MINING HEAVEN

Never dig straight down! You should mine in a diagonal line, so you're digging a staircase into the ground. Not only is this safer than risking a fatal drop into a cave, but it makes it easier for you to travel back out of the mine, too. You want to get your treasures back to the surface, don't you?

LIGHT UP THE MINES

Mining in the dark is about as good an idea as climbing a tree with your eyes closed. Not to mention that hostile mobs love low-light areas! Craft hundreds – yes hundreds – of torches and don't be shy about sticking them on the walls of your tunnels. The brighter, the better!

OUT OF ORE DEPTH

Finding useful ores will help you craft better weapons and armour to survive underground. In Minecraft, sea level is Y-62 and different ores are distributed at various levels. Using that as a guide, you'll find coal between 0 and 320, iron ore between levels -64 to 384 and diamond from -63 to 15.

BUBBLE COLUMNS

Waterfalls are a great way to travel up and down in caves. With an inventory full of materials, you don't want to meet hostile mobs as you find a way out. Create a bubble column by placing soul sand at the bottom of a volume of water. It'll transport you to the surface without reducing your air supply!

DISCOVER THE DEEP DARK

Minecraft's darkest biome is also one of its most lonely. Where better for a survival master to put their skills to the test? The deep dark is most likely to generate under mountainous areas. Although other hostile mobs don't spawn here, if you trigger the sculk sensors they will alert the warden to your presence.

NEED A LITTLE EXTRA HELP?

Things to be aware of in Minecraft's monster-filled mines ...

CREEP ALERT

Creepers are common underground and just love creeping up on you whilst you're busily mining away. Be wary!

WASH OUT

Struck water? Watch out! Swimming into dark water is easy, but finding a safe way back out can prove very tricky and lead to disaster.

I SPY

Using torches is a quick method of lighting up dark spaces, but keep some potions of Night Vision handy so you can wander in the dark, too.

STORAGE SOLUTIONS

Bring a chest in your inventory. If you gather more resources than you can carry, you can use it for extra storage space.

TIME KEEPER

Be aware of the time. One full day is 20 minutes, so work out when to avoid emerging into the night!

NOCTURNAL CHALLENGES

Day and night pose many different challenges when playing Minecraft. But if countless hostile mobs don't fill you with fear, then check out these challenges. You can only leave your base to complete them at night, so embrace your nocturnal side and give these tests a go!

Players	Difficulty	Perfect For	Items
1		Explorers	

RACE THE MOON

Build yourself a shelter and stick a beacon on top. Now, you're not allowed to build any more shelters and you can only gather resources at night. If you don't keep an eye on the moon and hurry back to your one shelter before the sun comes up, it's game over. How many days can you survive? Best of luck, nightwalker!

TOP TIP

It's against the rules to sleep in a villager's bed. Taking cover anywhere but your one base will result in your challenge coming to an end, my friend!

HOW WILL YOU RANK?

Copper
Survive three days

Iron
Survive five days

Diamond
Survive 10 days

Netherite
Survive 20 days

PHANTOM FUN

Fun? We're not sure about that. Phantoms start showing up when you haven't slept for three nights. In this challenge, you must play for three nights without sleeping, and then try to defeat one phantom each and every night, for 10 nights in a row. You can use any weapons you want and equip any armour. Trust us – you'll need it!

NIGHT TERRORS

When the sun goes down, equip your favourite weapon and head out with some friends. You must see how many hostile mobs you can hunt down and defeat before dawn. One little thing ... none of them will count if you don't get back to your meeting base before the moon disappears from the sky. The winner is the player who managed to hunt the most mobs!

TOP TIP

There are no limits on what you can use in this challenge. Loot as much as you can, and craft anything you choose to help you defeat as many hostile mobs as possible!

Players	Difficulty	Perfect For	Items
1-4	■■■ ■	*Hunters*	

HOSTILE MOBS CHALLENGE

Finding these challenges a little easy so far? Well, this one will test all your Minecraft skills and then some. Learning how to exist alongside hostile mobs might sound like a bizarre and dangerous proposition, but knowing how to deal with them will prepare you for future encounters.

Players	Difficulty	Perfect For	Items
1		The bravest of the brave	

GO HUNTING

Can you successfully capture and contain a whole bunch of hostile mobs? That's right ... you somehow need to trap them in enclosures. You can use any items or armour you choose. Go!

HOW WILL YOU RANK?

🥉 Copper

Collect three hostile mobs

⬜ Iron

Collect five hostile mobs

🔷 Diamond

Collect eight hostile mobs

⬛ Netherite

Collect 10 hostile mobs

Turn over for more ➡

CREEPS INCOMING

Dig a nice deep pit near your home and wait for night to fall. When it does, stand near the pit and swing a weapon to knock some hostile mobs inside it! Skeletons, zombies and creepers are common. Witches are slightly rarer, but could show up at any time. Enjoy your new holey home, monsters! Don't forget to build a ceiling once they're inside – or the sunlight will burn them.

ICE TO SEE YOU?

The stray is the grim answer to the question 'can skeletons get any worse?' If you simply must hunt one for this challenge, they're found in snowy biomes. Unlike skeletons, strays don't burn in sunlight and they fire arrows tipped with Slowness, making them hard to escape!

ENDERMITE BE A BAD IDEA

Defeat Endermen to get the Ender pearls they drop, then throw an Ender pearl to spawn an endermite. These tiny hostile mobs despawn within two minutes of spawning, unless you name them with a name tag. So spawn them in an enclosed space and name them!

SOAR LOSER

After three sleepless nights, phantoms will start hunting you, blissfully unaware that you're the one actually hunting them! They swoop down to attack, so consider building a structure that you can quickly leave and seal behind you. Did you know they're scared of cats? Use that!

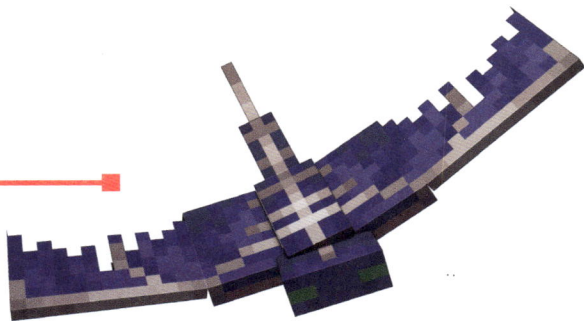

BOAT TRAP

Some mobs sit in boats, so place some and keep checking on them. When you find a mob sat in a boat, attach a lead and drag it – over land or sea – back to an enclosure. But be warned: in a boat, creepers can explode and skeletons can fire arrows. Maybe build the enclosure around them?

NEED A LITTLE EXTRA HELP?

Here's how to find some of Minecraft's other hostile mobs ...

PILLAGER
Pillagers can be found in pillager outposts near some villages. You might also encounter them as they patrol all across the Overworld.

SILVERFISH
This little mob spawns in mountains, igloo basements and woodland mansions, by infesting stone and deepslate blocks. Yuck.

SLIME
Slimes can spawn deep underground or in swamp biomes. You might hear their squelch noise before you see them!

SPIDER SENSE
Spiders are only hostile towards you when it's dark, so try to gather this mob when it's light outside and they're neutral.

JUST ADD WATER
Struggling to catch a drowned? Fill up the pit you're keeping a zombie in with water and they'll turn into a drowned. Easy!

NO MINING, NO CRAFTING!

It's time to see how you fare without doing either of the actions in Minecraft's name. Yep, no mining, no crafting and neither of them in the finale! In these difficult challenges, you can use anything you loot to help you make it to the End and defeat the Ender Dragon.

ZERO CRAFTING ALLOWED

The key for this one is lots of looting! Search villages for chests that'll hopefully give you a pickaxe (useful for clearing blocks, but remember, you can't craft with any resources you mine), a weapon and some armour. To get even as far as the Nether, you'll have to build your portal in place, using buckets of water and lava.

TOP TIP

You can find ruined Nether portals in the Overworld, which will save you lots of time. They have chests near them, too – which you can loot!

HOW WILL YOU RANK?

Copper	Survive in the Overworld
Iron	Reach the Nether
Diamond	Reach the End
Netherite	Defeat the Ender Dragon

Players	Difficulty	Perfect For	Items
1		Hardcore players	Whatever you can find – you can't craft any!

ZERO MINING ALLOWED

No mining? Seems impossible! But there are other ways to break up blocks. Try luring creepers towards any blocks you want mined and trigger their explosion, or search shipwrecks to maybe find TNT blocks. Don't forget you can craft this time – so forge yourself the best weapons and armour possible from whatever materials you gather!

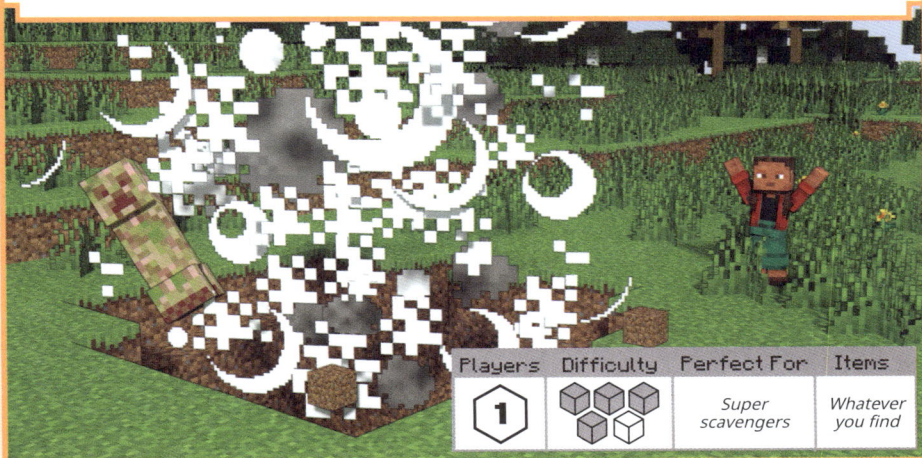

Players	Difficulty	Perfect For	Items
1		Super scavengers	Whatever you find

Players	Difficulty	Perfect For	Items
1		The most hardcore player in Minecraft history	All the luck you get!

TOP TIP

Look after your treasures! Remember, every resource you find in this task can't be crafted with or mined for. We'd recommend scavenging for the best tools you can find before risking any trips to the Nether and the End.

THE EPIC FINALE: NO MINING OR CRAFTING ALLOWED

Uh oh. You'll need to take everything you've tried in the previous two challenges and hope you have a lot of luck thrown in for good measure. Keep in mind all the things you can do: you can trade with villagers, loot chests, drink any potions you find and fight with whatever weapons you discover – good luck!

OCEAN LIVING

Living under the sea would be brilliant, wouldn't it? Dolphins for neighbours, no need to worry about uninvited Endermen popping up at your base? The Overworld's oceans are full of intriguing mobs and useful blocks that you'll find nowhere else!

Players	Difficulty	Perfect For	Items
1	◼◼◼	*Underwater adventurers*	◆ ◆ ◆

DIVE IN

This challenge isn't just about surviving under the surface, but building your own base underwater. Your ranking will depend on how fancy your building is. You must gather and build in Survival mode.

HOW WILL YOU RANK?

Copper
A single room base underwater

Iron
A multi-room base underwater

Diamond
A three room base over 10 blocks below the surface

Netherite
An underwater glass mansion with a tunnel to dry land

Turn over for more ➡

SUPPLIES

Before exploring underwater, we recommend you brew a potion of Night Vision and a potion of Water Breathing. A conduit will restore your oxygen and provide night vision, as well as causing damage to drowned, elder guardians and guardians within its range.

LOCATION

Before building your underwater home, try seeking structures, such as ocean monuments. Bring lots of weapons for the hostile mobs, but leave room in your pockets to gather lanterns and sponges. You'll also find prismarine, which can be used to build frames for a conduit.

SHELTER

Once you've picked a location for your underwater base, we'd recommend using glass blocks to build it first (you can always replace them later). Transparent glass will let the limited light in and make it much easier to see what you're doing. Plus, you can admire the sea life while you build. Bonus!

SUPPLIES

Remember those sea lanterns and sponges we told you to get earlier? Time to use them! Sea lanterns are super useful for brightening the place up, but sponges are even more handy, because they'll drain all the water out of your sealed base. Slurrrrp! Thanks, sponges.

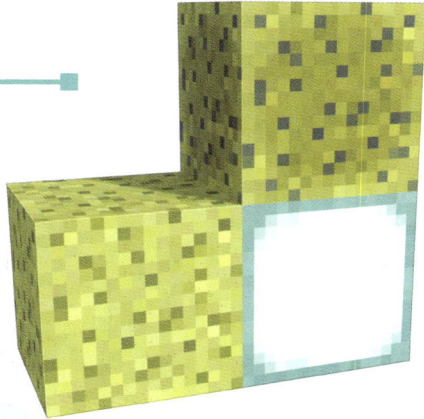

LOCATION

Having a base that's deep underwater is great for showing off, but make your first one in shallower waters. That way you won't waste so many potions of Water Breathing and can get back to land easily for more supplies. Once you've done that, try going for a deeper, more ambitious base!

NEED A LITTLE EXTRA HELP?

Here's how to make your underwater existence a little easier ...

SPONGE SMELTER
Dry out your wet sponges by placing them in a furnace with any fuel. They'll become dry and ready to soak up more water!

KEEP IT LIGHT
Sea lanterns are handy but rare. Once your base is water free, use other light sources such as lanterns and glowstone!

SAFE PASSAGE
Build a dry tunnel that leads all the way from your base to dry land. It'll take some time, but make ocean living easier!

TURTLE POWER
Wearing a turtle shell will grant you the Water Breathing effect for 10 seconds! This refreshes every time you surface for air.

FEROCIOUS FORK
A trident will make fighting hostile mobs underwater much easier. Sadly, they're a very rare drowned drop.

LIGHTING CHALLENGES

Minecraft is a bright and cozy game full of cute mobs! Until the lights go out ... then it can quickly turn into a terrifying experience. These challenges take advantage of Minecraft's spooky side and test your ability to play with limited vision. Wait ... did you just hear something?

BLAZE MAZE

In Creative mode, build a big maze out of obsidian blocks, with high walls and confusing routes (make sure you make a ceiling, too). Now place four chests in the maze with a diamond block in each one. Finally, spawn three blazes in the maze. They're the only source of light! Switch to Survival and put your friends in the maze. Who can get the most diamond blocks?

TOP TIP

Because your maze is so dark, more hostile mobs will spawn. So don't just keep your eye out for blazes. Watch for other hostile mobs, too!

Players	Difficulty	Perfect For	Items
2-4	▣▣▣	*Navigators and survivors*	None

SOUNDCRAFT

How well do you know Minecraft? So well you could play it in total darkness? For this challenge, you need to generate a new world using the superflat option and try to survive for 10 minutes with your eyes closed. Listen carefully now – was that the sound of a friendly pig or a much-less-friendly creeper?

Players	Difficulty	Perfect For	Items
1		Good listeners	Anything you want

TOP TIP

The warden is your main concern here, so running around to quickly place torches isn't the smartest strategy. Of course, you could always try and make a lot of noise around your friend so the warden finds them first ...

DEEP DARK BRIGHT-OFF

Find the deep dark biome in Creative mode, then fill all nine hotbar slots with torches and your friend's with redstone torches. Switch back to Survival and begin! Whoever places all their torches first, without anything nasty defeating you, wins!

Players	Difficulty	Perfect For	Items
2		Quiet players	

ROLEPLAY CHALLENGE

Playing Minecraft is brilliant with friends and there is so much fun to be had by taking on new and different roles. Feel free to jump into Creative mode to get the items you need, then start a roleplay adventure in Survival as a terrific or terrifying team!

Players	Difficulty	Perfect For	Items
1-6		Team players that work to achieve goals	

ROLE ON

We've created several different characters that you and your friends can play as. Who will play which role and, more importantly, how long can you maintain your new story campaign?

HOW WILL YOU RANK?

Copper

Stay in your roles for one day

Iron

Create an epic story using your roles for 10 days

Diamond

Play your roles for three months

Netherite

Play your roles for six months, then add new roles to take on

Turn over for more

THE POTION MASTER

This brilliant brewer has access to some truly powerful potions! They can start with any 26 potions of their choice and a brewing stand. They can throw negative potions at enemies and helpful ones at allies. Whoever picks this role better have brewing skills and a good aim.

THE DETONATOR

The riskiest choice of role! The detonator starts out with a flint and steel, 100 blocks of TNT, 20 fire charges, and 50 creeper spawn eggs, so we'd highly recommend staying on their good side. As the riskiest member of your team, they can be explosively handy, but very dangerous up close!

THE ROBIN HOOD

The player with the best aim should take this role, as they start with a bow with the Infinity enchantment. Their reputation for stealing from the rich means they also start with 100 emeralds. However, if a village gets raided, they have to stay and help the villagers survive the raid!

THE BEASTMASTER

You'll have to be good with animals and very brave to pick this one, as the beastmaster starts with 27 spawn eggs of any mobs they want. Friendly tip? Don't pick 27 wardens unless you never want your friends to speak to you again. Choose wisely, beastmaster!

THE ANGRY CHEF

The chef starts out with 20 meals of their choice (mmm, all the suspicious stews?) and an axe to chop wood as fuel. The chef is also the only one of your party allowed to cook, so be nice to them and keep the fuel flowing or you'll be eating raw chicken for dinner again!

NEED A LITTLE EXTRA INSPIRATION?

Here are five more roles you and your friends can take on ...

THE SPY
Starts with 10 potions of Invisibility and 10 potions of Night Vision. Perfect for those who prefer a sneaky approach to combat.

THE PILLAGER
Begin with a crossbow and 50 ravager spawn eggs. Risky! Don't expect to be welcomed at any villages in the near future.

THE TRADER
Starts with two llama spawn eggs, 20 emeralds and any five rare items. That's all you need to barter with!

THE ENDERMAN
Equip a diamond sword, a set of diamond armour and a totem of undying. You must attack any mob that looks directly at you!

THE PIG
Play Minecraft normally but make constant oinking noises, as you race around collecting pork chops to give to your friends as tasty offerings.

SNAIL CHALLENGES

What's the laziest way to play Minecraft? In bed eating cake? Maybe. Embrace your inner lazybones with these snail-paced challenges! How well can you survive when running and jumping are taken away from you? You can't take these on using flat worlds, so good luck!

Players	Difficulty	Perfect For	Items
1	◼◼◻	Slow and steady players	

NO RUNNING

What can you achieve in Minecraft without even breaking into a jog? We'd recommend mastering archery and using a sword before taking on this challenge. You'll need to defeat hostile mobs from afar. Try not to let them get too close, or they could quickly outnumber and outmuscle you!

TOP TIP

You can start with armour, and you'll want to learn to craft lots of it during this challenge. It's much harder to escape enemies without running, so you'll need it!

HOW WILL YOU RANK?

Copper
Survive the night

Iron
Reach the Nether

Diamond
Reach the End

Netherite
Defeat the Ender dragon

NO JUMPING

This one requires lots of careful planning and preparation. If you fall to the bottom of a deep pit, after all, it could be game over! Craft lots and lots of ladders so you will avoid such a fate. Remember, falling is allowed – just no jumping up even one block space!

Players	Difficulty	Perfect For	Items
1		Players who like to stay grounded	None

Players	Difficulty	Perfect For	Items
1		Masters of Minecraft	None

TOP TIP

The key to this challenge is to not be ... defeated. Move with caution and always try to avoid any risky situations. One wrong move and it could all be over!

NO RUNNING OR JUMPING

If you've managed the first two challenges, congratulations! Your 'prize' is this evil third challenge ... in which you can't sprint or jump. This will require all the experience you've had in the previous two challenges, so don't attempt this one first!

BITE-SIZED CHALLENGES 2

In a hurry to prove to your friends that you're the master of Survival mode? These competitive challenges will only take a few minutes to finish, but they'll need all your skills to master! Don't forget to be civil if you win – you don't want to ruin friendships just as fast!

NAME-OFF

Start in Creative mode. You and a friend now make 50 name tags with each of your names. Now, switch to Survival. You both have five minutes to name as many mobs after yourself as you can. Whoever names the most wins!

TOP TIP

Don't forget you can rename a mob that's already been named by your friend. Just don't get angry at us if they take this sly tactic badly!

HOW WILL YOU RANK?

Copper	*Name the most mobs*
Iron	*Name 10 more mobs than your opponent*
Diamond	*Name 25 more mobs*
Netherite	*Name 40 more mobs*

Players	Difficulty	Perfect For	Items
2-4		*Mob charmers*	50

52

OUT OF CONTROL

In the menu, select control settings. Change the controller, mouse or keyboard settings to reassign what all the buttons do. You and a friend must do this to each other's game, then swap back. You've got to see who can relearn the controls and make the most progress. You've then got 10 minutes to see who can build the most impressive structure!

Players	Difficulty	Perfect For	Items
2-4		Fast learners	None

TOP TIP

Change your strategy depending on which biome you spawn in. Ice biome? Get underwater. Mountain biome? Find a steep drop!

READY, SET, GAME OVER!

Usually in Survival mode, you're trying to survive (the clue is in the name). But this time, we want you and your friends to compete to see who can perish first! Will you sprint for the oceans? Dash into the dark forests and try to meet a hostile mob? Or dig straight down and hope for the worst? You'll have to fight all your survival instincts for this reckless challenge!

Players	Difficulty	Perfect For	Items
2-4		Risk takers	None

ONE COLOUR BUILDS

Normally, Minecraft bursts with different coloured blocks. But for these challenges, we want to see what you can build when you're restricted to just one colour. There are lots of clever ways to get variety into even a single-colour build!

GREY HOUSE

There are dozens of blocks and items with grey in their names. Can you build a great house that only uses them? It's tough, but there are some gorgeous grey blocks to play around with, including two types of glazed terracotta. Once you've created your grey masterpiece, extend your project to a bigger building, an entire village or even a biome!

Players	Difficulty	Perfect For	Items
1		Fans of building monochrome structures	Only grey blocks or items

TOP TIP

You never know where and when you'll find grey blocks. When you do, mine as many as you can carry to save you needing to go back for more later!

HOW WILL YOU RANK?

Copper
Build a basic grey house

Iron
Build a great grey castle

Diamond
Build an entire grey village

Netherite
Build a totally grey biome!

54

GOLDEN VILLAGE

What if a village struck gold? Find a village and replace as many of the buildings and paths as you can with gold. You'll have to be extremely rich to collect enough gold to pull off this one. We'd recommend heading to the badlands or the Nether to find it!

Players	Difficulty	Perfect For	Items
1-4	▣▣▢	Bling lovers	As much gold as you can find!

Players	Difficulty	Perfect For	Items
1-4	▣▣▣	Pink fans	Pink blocks, survival tools, stealthiness!

TOP TIP

Don't just carry pink stuff! This is one of the most dangerous biomes in Minecraft, so make sure you've got Night Vision potions, torches and survival tools, such as weapons and armour.

LIGHT THE DARKEST OF BIOMES

You'll need to be brave for this one! Take as many pink blocks as you can, ideally over 200, then locate a deep dark biome. It's time to give Minecraft's most sinister biome a pastel makeover. Try to replace over 200 blocks with lovely pink ones before the warden hears you!

CREATE ADVENTURES

You obviously like Survival and Creative, but have you tried Adventure mode? It is excellent for crafting unique maps for friends because it restricts what players can do in a Minecraft world. This gives you the power to craft incredible adventures for others to take on!

Players	Difficulty	Perfect For	Items
1		Survival storytellers	

GET CREATING

Your challenge here is to build a map in Adventure mode. The bigger and more demanding it is, the higher your rank will be. Turn the page to read some inspiration and see what's possible!

HOW WILL YOU RANK?

Copper

Build a map in Adventure mode

Iron

Craft an adventure that tests over three players

Diamond

Build an entire themed escape room

Netherite

Create a map that a player couldn't finish

Turn over for more ➡

USES

Effectively, Adventure mode stops players cheating during your adventures. If you've crafted a maze, they won't be able to knock down walls. If you've crafted a parkour map, they can't sneakily place their own platforms! You've removed the mining from Minecraft. So good luck, players ...

General

Advanced

Multiplayer

Cheats

Resource Packs

Behaviour Packs

CHANGE MODE

To activate Adventure mode, you must have cheats enabled in your world. Don't worry, this is easily found in the settings menu. Now enter the slash command /gamemode adventure. And just like that, no one can place or mine blocks. Er, don't do this until after you've built your map!

TEST TEST TEST!

The most important thing to do with your maps after you put them in Adventure mode is to make sure they're achievable! Run through them yourself, seeing if they can be completed without mining or placing blocks. Make any changes before you unleash them on your friends!

EXPLOSIVE

Players can't destroy blocks, but that doesn't mean the world is suddenly indestructible. Creepers can still blow up large chunks of the world when activated! You can stop hostile mobs spawning in the cheats – or perhaps leave them in and see if smart players can take advantage of this!

TOOLS FOR THE JOB

Players can still craft, but this is going to be much trickier when they can't mine for the resources they need. Make sure your adventure map includes the materials or the tools any players could use. It's not very fair to make them fight zombies unarmed … even if it would be funny to watch!

NEED SOME ADVENTURE INSPIRATION?

Here are a few more ideas to put into your adventures …

HOUSE OF HORRORS
Start players in the attic, then have them try to escape a house full of hostile mobs! Can anyone reach the exit?

HORDE MODE
Give players lots of weapons and armour. Stick them in a huge open arena full of hostile mobs! How long can they survive?

REDSTONE RACES
Set up some redstone fun, such as levers that open doors or move blocks in your maze. Maybe throw in some traps too!

LOOKING FOR LOOT!
Hide all of the materials to craft a weapon in chests. Players must find them all before hostile mobs attack.

CONSTANT CREEPERS
Build a maze with weapons hidden behind unbreakable walls. Players will need to activate creepers to get the weapons!

MOB BREEDING CHALLENGE

Beyond being an excellent source of cute baby animals, breeding mobs can provide you with food, items and lots of different crafting ingredients. It's also a peaceful pastime, and a perfect way to gather more of your favourite friendly animals!

Players	Difficulty	Perfect For	Items
1	■■■	Passive mob lovers	

START HERE

Let's make mob breeding a little more challenging? You have three in-game days to see how successful you can be. Turn over for helpful tips on being a brilliant breeder!

HOW WILL YOU RANK?

Copper

Breed three different passive mobs

Iron

Breed five passive mobs including one water-based mob

Diamond

Breed every passive mob

Netherite

Breed every passive mob and build enclosures for each

Turn over for more

SWEET HOME

Before tracking down the animals you need, make sure you have somewhere safe to lure them to. Build several secure pens so they can't escape from them – and hostile mobs can't get in. Make sure you avoid keeping mobs that are predators of other mobs in the same pen!

LOVE MODE

Mobs will only breed when they're in love mode. Clearly the way to a mob's heart is through its stomach, as feeding them the right food enters most mobs into love mode. Make sure the two mobs you're trying to breed are close to each other, then feed them both!

SUPPLIES

For goats, cows, mooshrooms and sheep, you'll need wheat to get them into love mode. For pigs you'll need carrots, potatoes or beetroot. Wheat seeds work for chickens, any raw or cooked meat works for wolves and hay bales work for llamas.

MORE SUPPLIES

Horses and donkeys sadly have expensive taste, so you'll need golden apples or golden carrots to breed them. The common carrot works fine for rabbits. Pandas like bamboo, foxes enjoy sweet berries and glow berries, whilst cats and ocelots like raw cod and raw salmon. Why aren't you gathering yet?

BEST OF THE REST

Don't forget your aquatic mobs! Axolotls like a bucket of fish and sea turtles enjoy seagrass. Hop back on land and give frogs slimeballs (eww), then head to drier biomes to give camels some cacti (owch) and bees some flowers (aww). Then you just need some torchflower seeds to breed a sniffer!

NEED A LITTLE EXTRA HELP?

Here's how to breed even the most committed solo mobs ...

HOT STUFF
Find a strider or a hoglin in the Nether! To breed them, use warped fungus for the strider, and crimson fungus for the hoglin. Yum!

CALM DOWN
Some mobs, such as wolves, horses, cats and donkeys will refuse to breed until you've tamed them first. How stubborn!

DONK-EH?
Breeding two horses gets you a foal and breeding two donkeys gets a donkey foal. Breed a horse with a donkey? You get a mule!

NO DINNER
For hopefully obvious reasons, keep your wolves and your foxes in separate pens to your chickens. Trust us, it won't end well.

BEEKEEPING
Bees have an irritating habit of ignoring the fences around your pen and flying off! Breed them somewhere with a roof to keep them in.

AMAZING MAZES

Got too many friends? After you've put them through the challenges on these pages, that won't be a problem. For these mazes, build high walls, winding routes, multiple entrances and a reward in the middle. Once you've made them in Creative mode and found a few friends, let the races begin!

STICKY SANDS MAZE

This maze is all about stopping players in their tracks! Make random sections of floor out of slime and honey blocks. Cover those in carpet and your maze runners won't know they'll be slowed down until they step on them! Put potions of Swiftness in chests – but put those chests near redstone traps that release lots of soul sand. Ha!

TOP TIP

As well as slowing players with hidden slime and honey blocks, insert dead ends and trick routes that will prevent them reaching the finish.

Players	Difficulty	Perfect For	Items
2-4	◼◼◼ ◻◻◻	*Speed runners*	🟧 🟩 ⬡

UNDERWATER MAZE

Let's take it underwater. Place chests containing potions of Water Breathing and potions of Night Vision. Craft some air pockets using sponge blocks so players can take a breather, and then spawn a few drowned! No placing conduits – that would be easy!

Players	Difficulty	Perfect For	Items
2-4	■■■/■■□	*Strong swimmers*	🧪🧪

TOP TIP

It's far more fair to give your friends a 15-second headstart. And don't just focus on one – remember, you want to stop them all finishing the maze!

Players	Difficulty	Perfect For	Items
2-4	■■■/■□	*Dungeon masters*	◈ ❄ ▢ ▦

DUNGEON MASTER MAZE

Build a huge twisty maze and add a layer of glass blocks on top. Fill your inventory with spawn eggs for hostile mobs! Switch to Adventure mode. Your friends have to run through the maze, whilst you stand above and try to stop them! When you spot one, smash the glass, and throw some spawn eggs in!

SCAVENGER HUNTS

There are treasures everywhere across the Overworld. Treasures like ... rotten flesh! And, er ... gravel! OK, two bad examples there. For these challenges, you'll need to find the treasures listed and successfully return to a set position to prove you're the ultimate scavenger.

SPAWN SEARCH

How quickly can you obtain some of Minecraft's more common items? Specifically, we want you to race to find spider eyes, string, rotten flesh and a helmet. You and your friends have to spawn into a new game and then sprint off to see who can get all four first, by any means!

Players	Difficulty	Perfect For	Items
2-4	■■□ / □■□	Speedy players	Nothing, but craft whatever you like

TOP TIP

This is one of the easiest challenges in the book. But it doesn't have to be. Add as many items to the list as you want, such as elytra!

HOW WILL YOU RANK?

Copper
Scavenge two of the items

Iron
Find all four items

Diamond
Scavenge all items quickest

Netherite
Find two of every item and still return first

DEEP SEA THRIVING

The Overworld's oceans are full of wonders to be found. They're also full of hostile mobs that are very keen for you to stay underwater ... forever. Who can collect the most ocean treasures? For this hunt, we want you to compete to get a trident, a heart of the sea and a nautilus shell. Whoever returns alive first with the items wins!

Players	Difficulty	Perfect For	Items
2-4	▣▣▢	*Ocean explorers*	

NETHER COMING BACK

Think you can achieve a truly hostile hunt? Then you and your friends must try jumping into a Nether portal and locating a Nether fortress! The clue is in the name – fortresses are no easy feat. We want you to search those chests until you find gold ingots, golden horse armour and Nether wart!

TOP TIP

Trying to fight everything the fortress throws at you is foolish. Let your friends worry about that while you run off to find those chests! Very sneaky of you ...

Players	Difficulty	Perfect For	Items
2-4	▣▣▣	*The truly brave*	

VEGETABLE CHALLENGE

Think Minecraft's tastiest mobs are too cute to eat? Too right they are! That's why these three challenges will put your vegetarian skills to the test. Survive these and you'll never need a pork chop again. Good news, pigs! You're off the menu for these challenges!

A FISHY DIET

Ease yourself into the joys of a restricted diet with a rule that you can't eat meat but you can eat fish. Yes, if it lives in the sea, bon appetit – er, but maybe don't eat drowned. This means you can't harm any passive or neutral mobs that live on land. But if it's in the sea, you can fill your belly!

TOP TIP

Cooked salmon is one of the best meals in Minecraft, restoring health and satisfying your hunger for a while. So scoff plenty of salmon!

HOW WILL YOU RANK?

Copper
Only eat meat in emergencies

Iron
Survive without meat for three days

Diamond
Survive on a fish-only diet for five days

Netherite
Survive by farming crops for 20 days

Players	Difficulty	Perfect For	Items
1		Seafood fans	None

VEGETARIAN RUN

For this challenge, you are not allowed to eat any sea creatures either. That means no harming anything passive or neutral that lives on land or in the sea. We'd recommend you get into baked potatoes. Or, if you're rich, golden carrots and apples, or tasty cookies!

Players	Difficulty	Perfect For	Items
1	■■□	Vegetarians	None

NO CREATURES HARMED

Hang on, true vegetarians don't go around attacking animals, no matter how hostile they are! So the ultimate vegetarian challenge would be to survive as long as possible without defeating a single neutral, passive or hostile mob. OK, we'll make one exception for the Ender Dragon – but otherwise, you've got to be friendly to all creatures great and ... well, horrible.

TOP TIP

You'll have to defeat a blaze to get the blaze rods you need to reach the End, so we'll make that an exception, too. Unless you know a way of getting a mob to defeat a blaze instead.

Players	Difficulty	Perfect For	Items
1	■■■	Peace lovers	None

ISLAND SURVIVAL

If you spawn on an island, you could begin again until you start elsewhere ... or you could try living out at sea. With less space and limited resources available, finding a way to survive might be difficult, but you'll discover techniques that will benefit you in other situations.

SURVIVE

If you haven't spawned on an island, switch to Creative mode to find one before switching back to Survival. How long can you survive without visiting the mainland? Keep reading for some tips on island living!

Players	Difficulty	Perfect For	Items
1		Solo adventurers	

HOW WILL YOU RANK?

🟧 **Copper**

Survive one day and night

⬜ **Iron**

Survive for five days

💎 **Diamond**

Survive for seven days and expand your island

⬛ **Netherite**

Make your island self-sufficient and survive for 30 days

Turn over for more ➡

RESOURCES

Breaking trees to get wood is how almost every Minecraft adventure starts. Start on an island with at least one tree, but don't use it up too quickly. Keep an eye out for saplings and plant replacement trees as fast as possible. Don't let wood go extinct!

FISHY SITUATION

Fishing is an easy way to get lots of food on your island, even without a fishing rod. A basic wooden sword is enough to take out a cod or salmon in one hit. Just keep an eye on your oxygen levels and make sure you watch out for drowned!

SHELTER

It can take a while for a sheep to spawn on your island so you can obtain wool to craft a bed. Don't wait to build a shelter! When night falls, you're going to want a safe hideaway from any hostile mobs, even if you are going to be staying wide awake all night long.

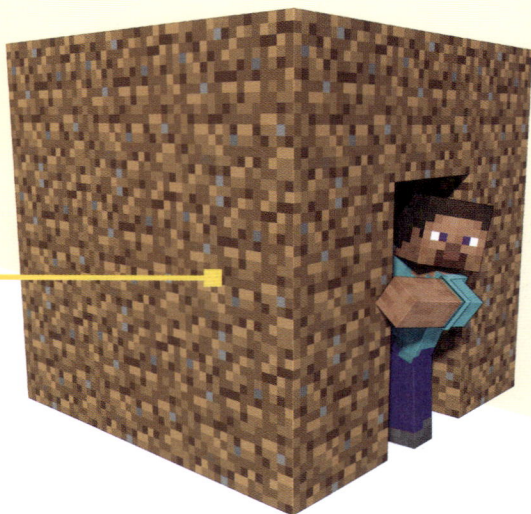

ANIMALS

It can be tempting to attack animals as soon as they spawn and gather their precious resources. Resist that temptation! You'll be better off building pens and farming them. Chickens will produce plenty of eggs. Once you've made shears, sheep will become an endless supply of wool.

DIG STRAIGHT DOWN

OK, not straight down, but who says you have to stay on the surface of the island? In the Overworld, you're almost always standing on top of a literal goldmine of precious resources. Make sure you've crafted a base and obtained a steady supply of food on the surface first though!

NEED A LITTLE EXTRA HELP?

Tips for making life on your island a tropical breeze ...

DROWNED
Fancy fighting the drowned? Lure them to the surface. They're easier to fight on land, where you won't have to worry about losing air.

BE RIGHT BACK!
One advantage to living on an island? Your respawn point is always nearby. If you're defeated, your stuff won't be far away!

EXPAND YOUR LAND
There are lots of dirt blocks underwater. Gather them and add land to your island so you have more space to use.

HAVE A LIE IN
Remember, hostile mobs lurk for a while in the mornings! Wait in your shelter until the sun has finished removing them.

NIGHT TERRORS
Sheep are the only exception to not defeating mobs. You need to craft a bed as soon as possible, or phantoms will pay you a visit!

PARKOUR CHALLENGES

Learning to run and jump with style is essential to surviving. How many times have you barely escaped a detonating creeper just in time? These parkour challenges will put your hopping skills to the ultimate test! It's time to run down these pages – fast!

TOP TIP

Try out your course in Creative mode before forcing your friends to try it in Survival. Don't debut it there until you're certain it can be completed.

HOW WILL YOU RANK?

Copper

Complete the course after many fails

Iron

Complete the course after two failed runs

Diamond

Complete the course after one failed run

Netherite

Complete the course on the first attempt

THE FLOOR IS (MOSTLY) LAVA

There's nothing like the threat of falling into fire to motivate your parkour players. For this first course, build platforms and fill the spaces in between with lava (we'd recommend building this in Creative mode). Start off with big platforms and small pools of lava, then make the platforms smaller and the lava lakes bigger!

Players	Difficulty	Perfect For	Items
2-4	▢▢▢	*Spring-footed players*	*None*

DON'T LOOK DOWN

The sight of bubbling lava can make even the most confident parkour pro into a jelly-legged stumbler. So why don't we throw some vertigo into the mix? This time, we want you to make a parkour course high up in the clouds! One missed jump and it's a looooooooong way down ...

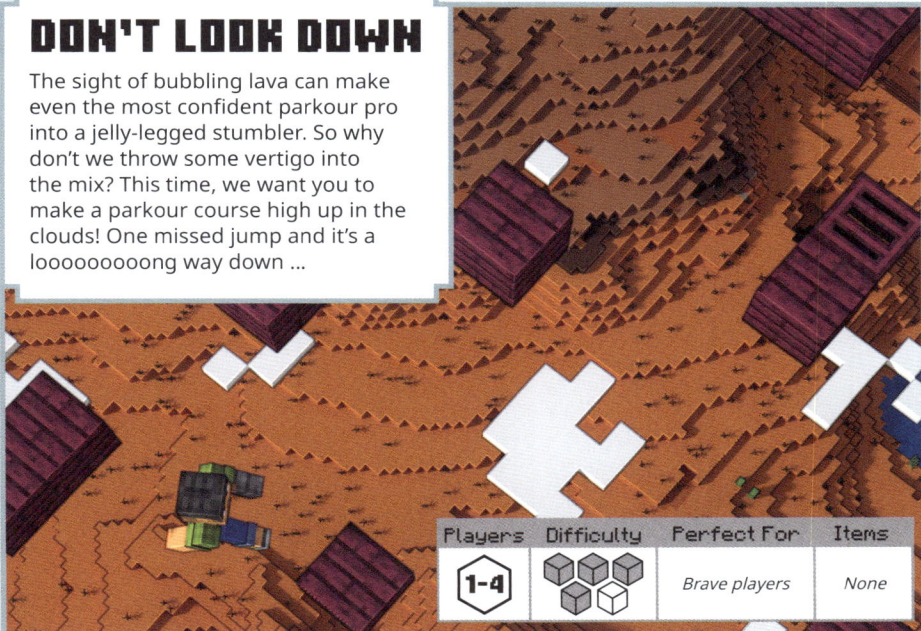

Players	Difficulty	Perfect For	Items
1-4	■■■	*Brave players*	*None*

TOP TIP

Phantoms will knock runners off the course. Although speed is essential, remind players that looking out for phantoms and trying to deter their attacks with arrows will help their cause.

KNOCK IT OFF

Your parkour courses would probably be easier if there were lots of friendly faces cheering your runners on ... but we're not here to make things easier, are we? That's why we want you to make a parkour course high in the sky and then use spawn eggs to surround it with phantoms! Can your runners successfully navigate the course without being pushed off by the soaring hostile mobs?

Players	Difficulty	Perfect For	Items
1-4	■■■	*Fighters*	🗡 🏹 🛡 🔱

BITE-SIZED CHALLENGES 3

Do you love a good challenge, but find yourself short on time?
Don't worry, we'll keep this intro as brief as possible. The following
challenges can all be achieved in just a few minutes – perfect for
timesavers and impatient Survival fans alike!

TOP TIP

Don't waste time giving each mob a portrait! It's easy enough to get several mobs in the same screenshot. Tick off the cow, sheep, chicken and pig in one shot and you'll be laughing.

HOW WILL YOU RANK?

Copper	10 mobs snapped
Iron	30 mobs snapped
Diamond	50 mobs snapped
Netherite	Every mob snapped (Um, how?)

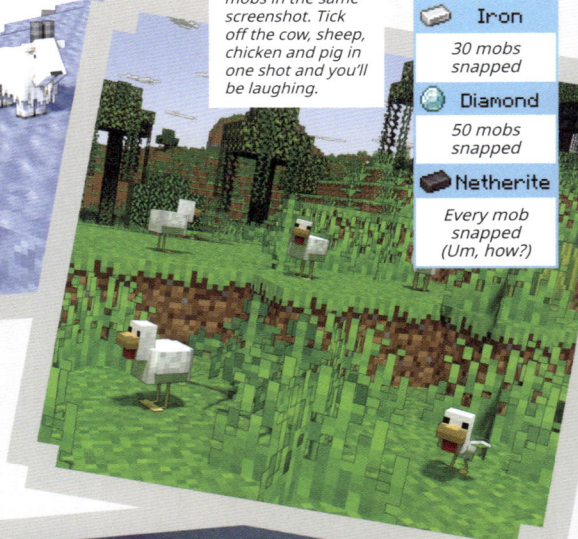

MOB SNAP!

Taking screenshots is a great way to share your favourite Minecraft memories with your friends. But how many memories can you make in just five minutes? For this challenge, we want you to get screenshots of as many mobs as possible in just 300 seconds!

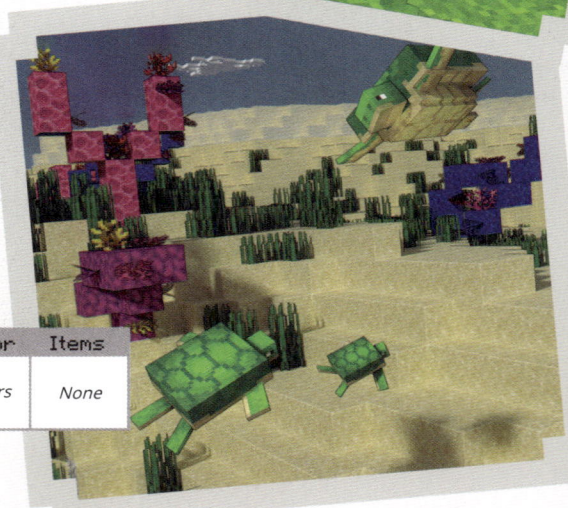

Players	Difficulty	Perfect For	Items
1	⬢⬢⬢	Photographers	None

SPREAD THE LOVE

To breed mobs, you need to feed them certain foods that will get them into love mode (see pages 62–63 for more). How many mobs can you breed in five minutes? Research their preferred foods before jumping into this lovely challenge. Come on piggies, eat up – we're on a deadline here!

Players	Difficulty	Perfect For	Items
1		Animal fans	

FILL YOUR INVENTORY

If you're carrying blocks or items that can stack 64 times, you can carry an incredible 2304 in your inventory – or more if you're using shulker boxes! Start a new game in Survival, then race your friends to see who can fill their inventory the most in just three minutes of play.

TOP TIP

It doesn't have to be three minutes! Decide a time and adjust it each round if you want to get more out of this challenge.

Players	Difficulty	Perfect For	Items
1-4		Hoarders	None

COLLECT EVERY PLANT

The dimensions of Minecraft have enough plant life to keep even the busiest gardener happy. At time of writing, 19 items and 38 blocks are considered plants! That's why we want you to embrace your green thumbs with these challenges. Er, not that we're saying you're grumpy, of course!

COLLECT EVERY PLANT

Build yourself a nice big greenhouse in Creative mode, then switch to Survival and see if you can fill it with every plant from Minecraft's dimensions. Start simple – you won't have too much trouble tracking down a grass block – and work your way up to the toughest plant life. We'd recommend saving ones like the chorus plant, which sadly likes to live in the End dimension, until the, well, end!

TOP TIP

Make frequent trips back to your greenhouse to deposit your obtained plants. If you're defeated out there and lose them all, you'll have to start the whole challenge over!

HOW WILL YOU RANK?

Copper	Collect 30 different plants
Iron	Collect 35 plants
Diamond	Collect 40 plants
Netherite	Collect them all

Players	Difficulty	Perfect For	Items
1		Explorers	None

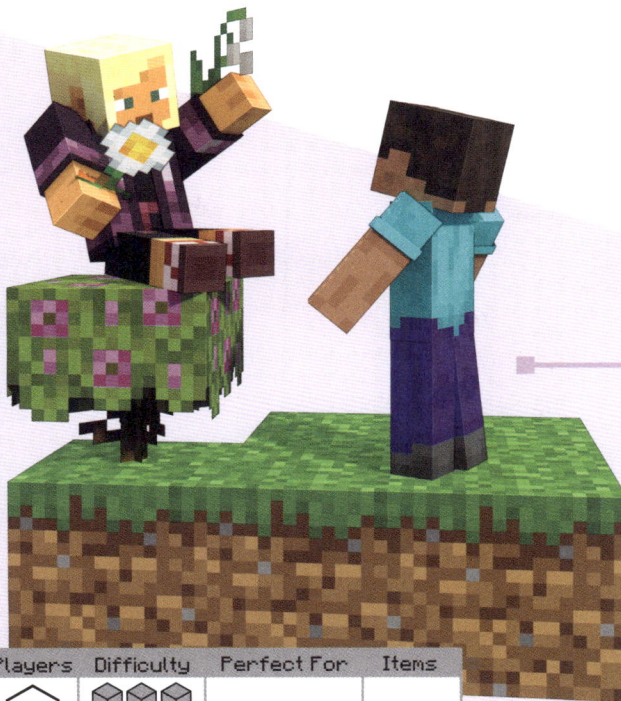

FASTEST GREEN FINGERS

Don't think gardeners are competitive? Clearly you've never had the pleasure of watching a gardening competition! For this challenge, we want you and your friends to compete to see who can obtain the most plants in 20 minutes. No repeats, no sabotaging other players, and no claiming that sheep you dyed green is a walking bush. That's the oldest trick in the book that no judge will fall for!

Players	Difficulty	Perfect For	Items
2-4		Quick collectors	None

TOP TIP

Use the plant-based blocks for the core structure of the build and save the majority of the items for decoration!

GREENEST HOUSE

We've all seen greenhouses made of glass, but what about a greenhouse that truly embraces nature? For this challenge, we want you to build the most impressive house you can ... using only plants and plant-based blocks! You've got 30 minutes until you and your friends will all judge each other's green creations!

Players	Difficulty	Perfect For	Items
1-4		Builders	Only plants!

UNDERGROUND CHALLENGES

Exploring the Overworld's underground is essential for survival success and these challenges are a great way to expand your underground experience. How many people have attempted these, gone below the surface and never returned? Er, we'd rather not say. Have fun

HOW LONG CAN YOU GO?

Go underground. In the settings menu, under world coordinates, toggle a switch that says show coordinates. Three numbers will appear on the top-left side of the screen. The left and right numbers show where you are positioned in the world. We want you to go as far as possible in one direction! You'll face hostile mobs and a very real lack of food!

TOP TIP

The y number shows your elevation, which is how high or low you are. You can go up and down as long as you avoid going above ground!

HOW WILL YOU RANK?

Copper	
100 distance	
Iron	
150 distance	
Diamond	
250 distance	
Netherite	
500 distance	

Players	Difficulty	Perfect For	Items
1		Burrowers	None

80

CREEPER CAVES

Players	Difficulty	Perfect For	Items
1	▦▦▦	Quick movers	50

Start in Creative mode. Put 50 creeper spawn eggs in your inventory. Switch to Survival mode and turn on the world coordinates. Now we want to see how low you can dig using only your explosive new pets! That's right, to explore, you'll need to summon creepers, trigger them and then run away and hope they blow up a nice new route for you – no armour allowed!

MOLE LIFE

Start a new game and immediately punch yourself a hole in the ground until you access some underground space. Your mission is to see how long you can survive living down there! You must begin with nothing, but can craft anything!

TOP TIP

Look out for mineshafts. They could contain chests with sources of food stored inside.

Players	Difficulty	Perfect For	Items
1	▦▦▦	Sun haters	None

MOJANG EASTER EGGS

Name tags are a fun way to give your favourite pet mobs cute nicknames! They're also a great way for the Minecraft developers to sneak in some fun Easter eggs. Did you know that naming mobs can have some delightfully odd side effects? What a laugh!

RAINBOW SHEEP CHALLENGE

Use an anvil to make your name tag say 'jeb_' then use it on a sheep. You'll get a rainbow sheep with wool that constantly changes colours! This is a reference to Minecraft developer Jens 'Jeb' Bergensten. How many sheep can you give the rainbow treatment?

Players	Difficulty	Perfect For	Items
1		Creative shepherds	

TOP TIP

Remember, each time you give a tag a name, it'll cost you 1 experience point. Make sure you have enough experience before seeking out sheep!

HOW WILL YOU RANK?

Copper	10 rainbow sheep
Iron	25 rainbow sheep
Diamond	50 rainbow sheep
Netherite	100+ rainbow sheep

TOAST CHALLENGE

Sorry to disappoint our hungrier readers, but there's no toast in Minecraft (and don't bother trying to throw bread into lava – it doesn't work). But if you use a name tag to call a rabbit Toast, it'll get a cute new black-and-white pattern. This was done by a Minecraft developer as a tribute to an actual missing rabbit of the same name. How many rabbits can you make into Toast in 10 minutes?

Players	Difficulty	Perfect For	Items
1	◼◻◻	Animal lovers	

DINNERBONE CHALLENGE

If you use a name tag to call a mob Dinnerbone, it'll flip upside down! This is a reference to Nathan 'Dinnerbone' Adams, a Minecraft developer who likes to have his profile picture the wrong way round. But how many different mobs can you flip in your Survival Overworld? The previous two challenges were pretty easy, but this will really test your survival skills!

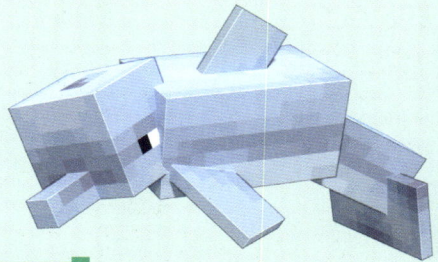

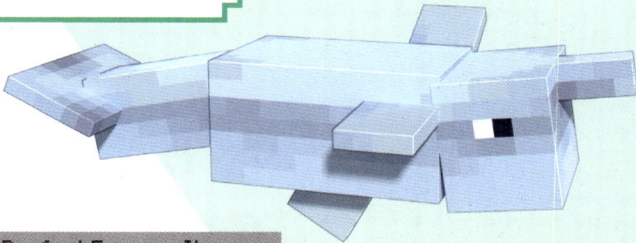

TOP TIP

Make sure you're stocked up on name tags, so you can use them whenever you stumble across each new mob – some will take time to find!

Players	Difficulty	Perfect For	Items
1	◼◼◼◻◻	Completionists	

200 BLOCKS ONLY!

For this trio of challenges, you need to make every block count. You can only use 200 blocks per challenge, so use them wisely. 200 may sound like a big number, but you'll be surprised how quickly it falls to zero if you don't craft with care!

TREEHOUSE CHALLENGE

You can only place 200 blocks, so why not take advantage of the blocks that are already there? Find somewhere with dense trees, such as a roofed forest biome, then build your home around them! Use sections of the trees as part of your walls, prune the leaves so you can have leafy windows. For it to qualify as a house, you must be safe from hostile mobs inside it at night. Good luck!

Players	Difficulty	Perfect For	Items
1		Nature lovers	200 blocks and nothing else

TOP TIP

Use tree canopies or even the ground itself for the flooring of your treehouse. Save your block usage for filling in any gaps!

HOW WILL YOU RANK?

Copper

Successfully build a house with your 200 blocks

Iron

Build a house using only 150 blocks

Diamond

Build a house using only 100 blocks

Netherite

Build a house using only 50 blocks

ONE OF EVERY BLOCK

Build a house using 200 blocks with a catch ... you can only use each block once! The challenge here is to make something that looks good even though builds that use too many different blocks often look a bit messy and chaotic. Pick your 200 favourite blocks, get crafting and remember – no repeats allowed!

Players	Difficulty	Perfect For	Items
1-2		Decorators	200 unique blocks

BAD BRIDGE CHALLENGE

Building bridges is a great way to safely explore the highest peaks of the Overworld. But what if you only had 200 blocks? A chasm that's only 50 blocks wide shouldn't be too tough – but 150 blocks would be. Using your 200 blocks, try building a bridge across a chasm that's at least 150 blocks wide and 100 high!

Players	Difficulty	Perfect For	Items
1		Those who aren't scared of heights	200 blocks that aren't affected by gravity. Don't use sand for this one!

TOP TIP

Got holes in your bridge so it stretches farther? Remember, players can only jump 1.25 blocks when walking. You can get further sprint-jumping, but you'll need space to sprint!

COMMUNITY CHALLENGES

There is an amazing online Minecraft community that is always coming up with challenges. Frankly, they love coming up with ideas that will inspire your own creativity and terrify you in equal measure. Especially if you attempt the infamous 100 days challenge. Gulp. Thanks, you lot!

Players	Difficulty	Perfect For	Items
1		Mega Minecrafters	Anything the challenge says you can use

HOW WILL YOU RANK?

Copper
Try one community challenge

Iron
Try three community challenges

Diamond
Try five community challenges

Netherite
Try all six community challenges

TRY THEM ALL

On the following pages, we've collected some of the most popular community challenges! How many will you try and how far can you take them?

Turn over for more ➡

HARDCORE

Though only available in Java Edition, Hardcore is a mode in which you don't respawn once you're defeated – it's game over. Your saved world will be gone! This is easily replicated in Bedrock by deleting your save file when you perish. Use anything available to complete the game without failing once? You couldn't ... could you?

NOMAD CHALLENGE

Living as a nomad in Minecraft is tricky. You can't build a home and you can't use chests! You can still craft and sleep in beds, but never in the same biome twice – you must keep moving and have your wits about you. An excellent challenge for those wanting to explore the Overworld!

SINGLE BIOME CHALLENGE

Pick a biome and see how long you can survive without leaving it. Easy in a forest biome, but a bit of a nightmare in the desert. And you're braver than us if you attempt it in the Nether. Start with nothing, but craft anything you choose – as long as it's made from resources found in the biome.

100 DAYS

Thought the Hardcore challenge was too easy? First off, you're amazing. Second, the community agreed and they have added this nasty twist – not only do you have just ONE life, but you have to finish Minecraft in 100 in-game days or under. Only the most determined will beat this one!

HAD ENOUGH

After so many survival challenges, why not treat yourself to some time in Creative mode? You can't perish, you can fly and you have access to every block and item you could ever want. Start a new world and play your way for 30 minutes to see what you can create!

FANCY SOME EXTRA CHALLENGES?

Wow, we're almost done? Not before you try these final five ...

TNT CASTLE
Can you build a castle entirely out of one of Minecraft's most dangerous blocks? Just keep creepers far away!

PERMANENT RECORDS
Can you track down every single music disc in the game? No other challenge will sound quite as sweet as this one does!

NETHER AGAIN
How many mobs can you force through a Nether portal and into the Overworld? Now why would you do that?

MOVING VILLAGE
If you slowly replace homes and gather the place up, what's stopping you from moving a village deep underground?

CREATE YOUR OWN
Hey, why should we do all the work? See if you can come up with some unique survival challenges of your own!

VARIATION CHALLENGES

Now that we've taken on a whole Overworld of survival challenges, all that's left to do is say goodbye ... Sorry, what's that? You want us to mash together some of them to create new nightmare combination challenges? That's brave. Proceed with extreme caution ...

GHASTLY SKY PARKOUR

Using the knock it off challenge from page 75, create a parkour course high up in the Nether and spawn ghasts instead of phantoms. The ghasts will shoot fireballs at players, which will either knock them off or break the course itself! Will anyone make it across safely?

TOP TIP

Players can equip a stack of any block they choose and use them to replace any sections of track that ghasts destroy.

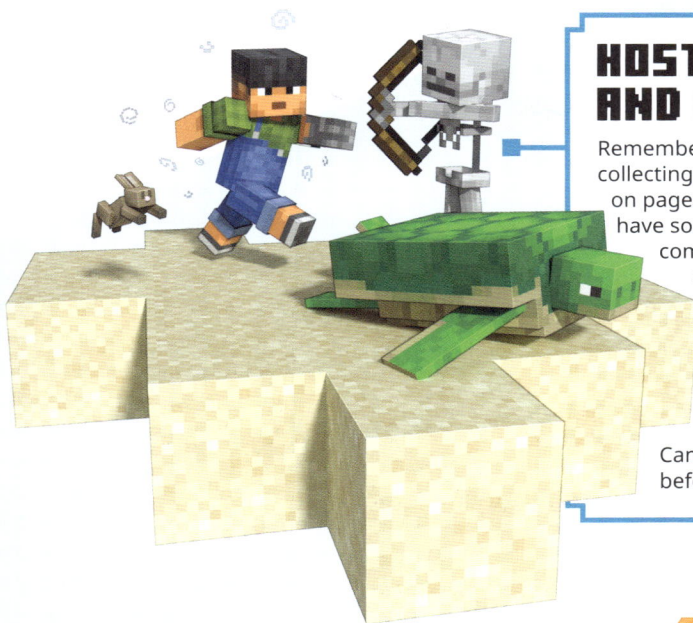

HOSTILE MOBS AND POTIONS

Remember when you tried collecting every hostile mob on pages 34 to 37? Let's have some, er, fun by combining this with the slowpoke challenge on page 18. That's right, you must try to collect hostile mobs whilst under the influence of a potion of Slowness. Can you collect any before being defeated?

NETHER CONTROLS

Two of the toughest challenges in this book were starting a new game in the Nether on pages 20-23 and learning new gameplay controls on page 53. Whatever could be harder? Doing both of those at the same time! Surviving in the Nether is hard enough, without the randomness of a new controller layout. Equip some armour and try to survive for 10 minutes!

TOP TIP

Quickly try to determine which controls will move you away from danger, and swing your arms to defeat any hostile mobs!

UNDERWATER AT NIGHT

Building an underwater base is difficult enough without any extra restrictions, so imagine also taking on page 33's night terror challenge! That's right, build by day then head out of your underwater base each night to hunt underwater hostile mobs. You've got three in-game days. The winner is the player who defeats the most mobs and has a functioning underwater base to return to.

ROLEPLAY AND CONQUER

Pages 46-49 were all about having fun with your friends whilst taking on different roleplaying challenges. Let's turn that on its head. Now, you must all take on roles as part of different settlements that want to defeat each other. Who can build a base capable of defending against all the attacks from your friends turned enemies?

ISLAND ANIMAL LOVER

On page 70-73 we challenged you to survive on an island for as long as possible. Now imagine trying that whilst also never harming a single mob! Will you become the Overworld's most famous farmer by somehow managing to plant enough crops on your island?

GOODBYE

Welcome to the end of the book! Did
you finish every challenge? Really?
Honestly? Goodness! You must be a
Minecraft Survival mode master now.
Congratulations! We hope the challenges
in this book helped you find new ways to
play on your own and with your friends.

Can you believe that this book has
only scratched the surface of what's
possible in the game? Explore the
Overworld, meet its mobs, trade with
its villagers, survive its monsters and
never stop thinking about how a cleverly
constructed challenge can breathe new
life into classic adventures. Why not keep
a record of any challenges that you
create yourself?

And if there was a challenge you couldn't
do in this book, that's fine – adjust it!
Change it! Improve it. The joy of Minecraft
is that you can play it however you like
and craft it into the perfect experience
for you. So keep looking for fresh
challenges and thanks for reading!